DK READERS

Level 2

Level 3

Level 4

A Note to Parents

DK READERS is a compelling program for beginning readers, designed in conjunction with leading literacy experts, including Dr. Linda Gambrell, Director of the School of Education at Clemson University. Dr. Gambrell has served on the Board of Directors of the International Reading Association and as President of the National Reading Conference.

Beautiful illustrations and superb full-color photographs combine with engaging, easy-to-read stories to offer a fresh approach to each subject in the series. Each DK READER is guaranteed to capture a child's interest while developing his or her reading skills, general knowledge, and love of reading.

The four levels of DK READERS are aimed at different reading abilities, enabling you to choose the books that are exactly right for your child:

Level 1 – Beginning to read
Level 2 – Beginning to read alone
Level 3 – Reading alone
Level 4 – Proficient readers

The "normal" age at which a child begins to read can be anywhere from three to eight years old, so these levels are only a general guideline.

No matter which level you select, you can be sure that you are helping your child learn to read, then read to learn!

LONDON, NEW YORK, MUNICH,
MELBOURNE, and DELHI

Project Editor Esther Ripley
Art Editor Nicola Liddiard
Senior Art Editor Cheryl Telfer
Managing Editor Deborah Lock
DTP Designer Almudena Diaz
US Editor Regina Kahney
Production Shivani Pandey
Picture Researcher Marie Osborn
Jacket Designer Chris Drew
Illustrator Peter Dennis
Indexer Lynn Bresler

Reading Consultant
Linda B. Gambrell, Ph.D

First American Edition, 2002
03 04 05 10 9 8 7 6 5 4 3 2
Published in the United States by DK Publishing, Inc.
375 Hudson Street, New York, New York 10014

Published in Great Britain by Dorling Kindersley Limited.

Library of Congress Cataloging-in-Publication Data
Garrett, Leslie, 1964-
  The story of Muhammad Ali / by Leslie Garrett.
  —1st American ed.
  p. cm—(Dorling Kindersley readers. Level 4)
  ISBN 0-7894-8516-8—ISBN 0-7894-8517-6 (pbk.)
  1. Ali, Muhammad, 1942—Juvenile literature. 2. Boxers (Sports)—
United States—Biography—Juvenile literature.
  I. Title. II. Dorling Kindersley readers. 4, Proficient readers.
GV1132.A44 G37 2002
796.83'092--dc21   2001037082

Color reproduction by Colourscan, Singapore
Printed and bound in China by L Rex Printing Co., Ltd.

The publisher would like to thank the following for
their kind permission to reproduce their images:
Position key: c=center, t=top, b=bottom, l=left, r=right.

Allsport: 2, 5 main image, 20; Jack Atley 42; Kendra Lenhart 39b;
American News: 47b; Associated Press AP: 7, 8tl; Corbis: 4, 9br, 10tr,
16tr, 16br, 19, 22tl, 23t, 24, 29b, 29t, 33, 34, 35, 38, 39t, 41t; Courier
Journal: 12tr, 41br; Empics Ltd: 14tl, 23b, 34b; John Frost Historical
Newspapers: 27t; Ronald Grant Archive: Howard L Bingham 36b;
Hulton Archive: 14b, 21br, 21t; Brian Hamill, Archive Images 5cr;
Evening Standard 36t; Monty Fresco 43b; The Observer 30; Popperfoto:
9, 15, 25, 26, 45, 46t, 47tr, 47cl; Rex Features: 18, 40, 43cl, 44; Life
Magazine 32; Topham Picturepoint: 13, 22b, 27b; Vin Mag Archive: 37.
Jacket: Hulton Archive: front jacket c, front jacket r.
Popperfoto: front jacket cr.
All other images © Dorling Kindersley Limited.
For further information see: www.dkimages.com

see our complete product line at
www.dk.com

Contents

DK READERS

PROFICIENT READERS 4

THE STORY OF
MUHAMMAD ALI

Written by Leslie Garrett

DK Publishing, Inc.

History of boxing
English boxing champion John Broughton first set out the rules of boxing in 1743. He also introduced padded mittens for fighters – the first boxing gloves.

Heavyweights
Boxers are put into divisions according to their weight. The lightest are strawweights and the heaviest are heavyweights – boxers who weigh at least 190 pounds (86 kilograms).

The road to greatness

Cassius Clay should have been terrified. It was February 25, 1964, and the 22-year-old boxer was facing the biggest fight of his career. Few rated his chances against his opponent – Sonny Liston, the current Heavyweight Champion of the World. But Cassius stayed cool – he had been dreaming about winning the title since he was 12 years old.

Who was Cassius Clay? He was a fighter with such speed and agility that he made boxing look beautiful. "I am the greatest" was his favorite boast. Time proved him right – he went on to take the title three times.

But Cassius was also a man of faith who fought battles outside the ring. He changed his name to Muhammad Ali and became a symbol of pride and strength to black people. Ali ended up as one of the most adored athletes of all time.

Sonny Liston

Heavyweight champion Sonny Liston had a deadly jab and a reputation as a bully. He had won his title in a match that lasted just two minutes and six seconds.

Ali's style

No one had ever seen a boxer quite as agile as Ali. While most boxers stood and slugged it out with their fists, Ali danced out of the way of punches.

5

Prankster
Cassius loved pranks. One of his favorites was to hide in a closet with a sheet over his head ready to jump out and scare his family.

Little brother
Younger brother Rudy also took up boxing when he was older, but he did not have the talent and drive of his big brother.

Humble beginnings

The first son born to Odessa and Cassius Clay Senior, on January 17, 1942, turned out to be a lively baby. The little boy, named Cassius after his father and grandfather before him, could pack a punch at just six months of age. Lying alongside his mother, he stretched out his little fist and knocked her in the mouth, loosening a front tooth.

The Clays lived in a modest bungalow among other black families in Louisville, Kentucky. Cassius's father painted signs and murals, and his mother sometimes worked as a maid for white families. When Cassius was two, his younger brother, Rudolph Valentino, was born.

Young Cassius was a prankster and always the center of attention.

This Kentucky school used armed guards to bar black children.

But like any black child of his generation, Cassius was aware that he did not share the same privileges as white children in his hometown.

Segregation laws were in place, and black people were routinely kept out of restaurants, stores, schools, and neighborhoods reserved for whites only. At an early age, Cassius began to question why black people had to suffer these injustices.

Segregation
US segregation laws were designed to keep blacks separate from whites. Black people were not allowed to eat in "whites only" restaurants, attend white schools, sit with white people on buses, or even use the same bathrooms.

Joe Martin
As well as training boxers, Joe Martin produced *Tomorrow's Champions*, a local TV program that showcased their talents.

At age 12, Cassius Clay's pride and joy was his new bicycle. One day it was stolen, so Cassius went to report the theft to Joe Martin, a police officer who trained young boxers at a local gym. Cassius was furious and vowed he would "whup" whoever had taken his bike.

"Well, do you know how to fight?" asked Martin. "Perhaps you ought to learn first."

Excited by what he had seen at the gym, Cassius soon went back and began to box.

He was not a natural boxer, but he was disciplined and determined and spent hours jumping rope and pounding a punching bag.

Just six weeks later, Cassius narrowly won his first bout against another 12-year-old and promptly announced that he would soon be the "greatest of all time."

A year or two later, Martin began to believe it. Quick-footed Cassius was the most talented boxer he had ever trained.

Sheer talent
At first Cassius was awkward in the ring and easily beat, but before long he had developed speed and amazing reflexes.

Diet and training
Cassius got up at dawn to run several miles and then had a quart of milk with two raw eggs for breakfast. He never drank soda – just water with garlic.

Golden boy

By the time Cassius graduated from Louisville Central High School, he had fought more than 100 bouts and lost only 8. He had also won six Golden Gloves tournaments and two national championships.

Golden Gloves
Amateur boxers competed in Golden Gloves tournaments, which were inter-city competitions sponsored by athletic clubs and recreation centers.

Joe Martin suggested that the 18-year-old should try for a place on the US Olympics team.

Cassius got through the trials, but persuading him to fly to the 1960 Olympics in Rome, Italy, was another matter – the boxer was terrified of flying. Finally, Cassius boarded the plane in an army-surplus parachute and wore it throughout the flight.

Poetry
Cassius wrote a poem to celebrate his Olympic win: "To make America the greatest is my goal; So I beat the Russian and I beat the Pole…"

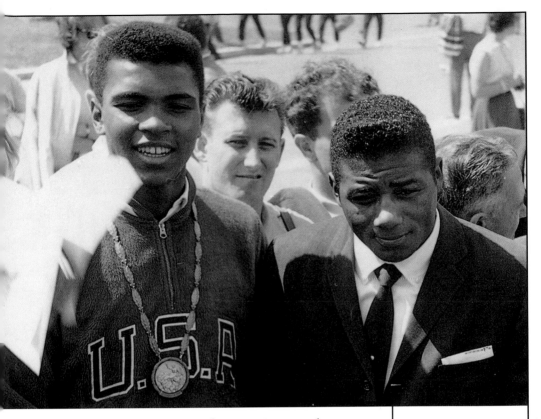

Cassius was a charmer at the Olympics, entertaining everyone with silly poems about his dazzling future. He got to the heavyweight final with ease and then beat a Polish boxer to win the gold medal.

Wilma Rudolph, a gold medallist and great friend, was amused because Cassius refused to be parted from his medal. "He slept with it. He went to the cafeteria with it. He never took it off," she said.

Wilma Rudolph
US sprinter Wilma Rudolph won three gold medals for running at the Rome Olympics.

On parade
Cassius was driven through Louisville in a 25-car motorcade. A banner at his old school read "Welcome Home Champ!"

Louisville celebrated the return of its hometown hero in style and held a parade in honor of Cassius Clay. But Cassius was increasingly troubled by the way black people were treated in US society.

Soon after he got back from Rome, he went to a restaurant with a friend and ordered a hamburger and a milkshake.

The waitress took their order and then came back to say that she could not serve them.

"But this is our Olympic gold medallist," said Cassius's friend. The white owner of the restaurant said he didn't care who it was – they were not going to be served. He wanted them out.

Cassius left, shamed and angry. Even though he had won gold for his country, he was still refused entry to some places because he was black.

Boxing had been a fast way for Cassius to make it in the US, but now he resolved to find ways to help all black people in their fight for freedom, justice, and equality.

Freedom fighting
The civil rights movement was gaining ground, with black people taking to the streets in organized protests to demand the same rights and privileges as white citizens.

Big Spender
Cassius did not believe in saving money and liked to spend lavishly on his family. His mother (right) and sister-in-law turned up at matches wearing beautiful furs.

Predictions
Cassius became so good at predicting how many rounds his opponents would last he made up a chant: "They all must fall in the round I call."

Poetry in motion

Not long after his return from the Olympics, Cassius turned professional, backed by a group of millionaires from Louisville. He was given a $10,000 bonus for signing the contract – a huge sum of money in the 1960s. Then Cassius won his first professional fight and picked up another check for $2,000.

Cassius continued to win, usually by knockouts, and continued to boast. He took to predicting with uncanny accuracy the round in which each opponent would fall.

Nicknames
The boxer's nonstop boasting irritated some of the old-time sports reporters, who nicknamed him Mighty Mouth and Louisville Lip.

Many people loved the young boxer's bravado – but just as many wished that he would shut up.

The truth was that Cassius was as much an entertainer as a boxer. "All that 'I'm the greatest' and 'I'm the prettiest'…yeah, I was acting," he admitted years later.

Pretty boxer
Cassius believed that if a boxer had speed and agility he need never get hit. He vowed that he would "stay pretty" right through his boxing career.

15

There was one fight Cassius wanted more than all the rest – against the Heavyweight Champion of the World, Sonny Liston. But first he had to get Liston's attention.

Cassius had a bus painted with slogans: "The World's Most Colorful Fighter – Liston Will Go in Eight" and set out for Liston's home in Denver, Colorado. He made sure the press would be waiting for him.

Crowds of reporters watched as Cassius stood on the curb yelling, "Come on out, Liston. I'm going to whip you right now."

Liston was furious, but he had a criminal record and didn't want to start any trouble. He was also confident of a victory against this big-mouthed boaster, so he told his representatives to agree to a title fight against Cassius Clay.

Bear baiting
For a stunt, Cassius took a rope to catch the "big bear" Liston, and a trainer carried a jar of honey.

In the weeks leading up to the fight, Cassius goaded Liston every chance he got, calling him a "big ugly bear" and a "chump."

Weigh-ins
Boxers are weighed shortly before a fight to make sure they are in the correct division.

However, at the weigh-in before the fight, the young boxer looked wild-eyed and out of control, lunging at Liston and shouting. Cassius Clay was acting crazy. Was he terrified?

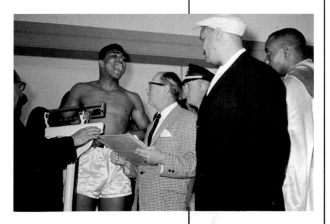

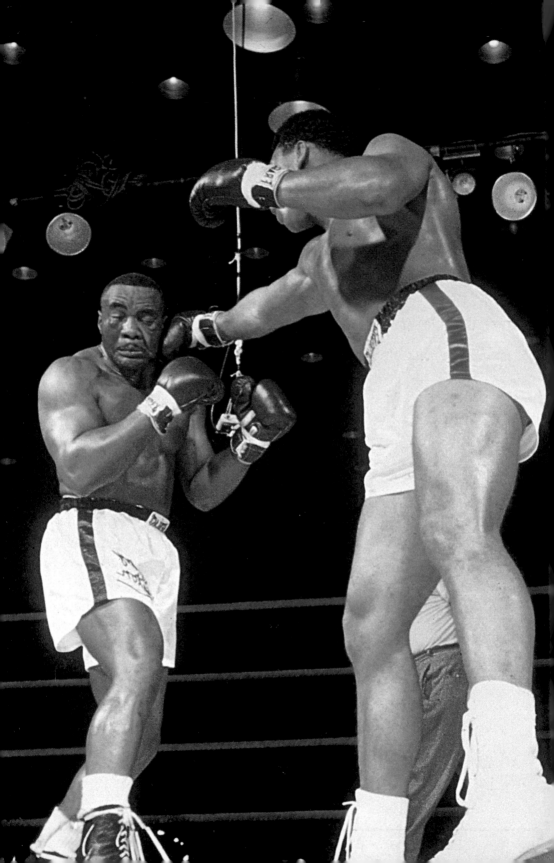

At 10 p.m. on February 25, 1964, the ring announcer reached for his microphone to welcome boxing fans to the Miami Beach Convention Hall for the Heavyweight Championship Title fight between Cassius Clay and Sonny Liston.

Cassius climbed into the ring and began to bounce and jab in his corner. Liston fixed him with a menacing stare. Cassius stared back.

Round one: at the sound of the bell, Cassius Clay began to canter clockwise around the boxing ring. His opponent lumbered after him, repeatedly swinging punches and missing – the normally light-footed champion was looking awkward.

As Cassius finished the first round the clear winner, announcer Joe Louis told the amazed audience: "I think we've just seen one of the greatest rounds we've had from anybody in a long time."

Championship belts
In the early days of boxing, jeweled bronze belts were given to boxers by rich patrons. In the 1920s, a boxing journal decided to present a belt to each world champion.

Joe Louis
The announcer, Joe Louis, was a former heavyweight champion and Cassius's childhood hero. He won the title in 1937 and held it until 1948.

A good trainer makes sure that his fighter is fit enough for a long match, yet is not burned out by too much training.

Liniment on the gloves
After the fight, there was speculation that Liston put liniment on his gloves to blind Cassius temporarily. However, it may have been unintentional.

Cassius continued to dance away from the heavy punches, and by round four, Liston was looking shaken up and desperate. He had expected an early knockout and so had not trained for a lengthy fight. Cassius was supposed to be terrified.

But in the fourth round, Cassius seemed to be in trouble and was rubbing his eyes with his gloves. When he got back to his corner, he was in agony. "I can't see!" he yelled to his trainer. "Cut off the gloves."

But the gloves stayed on. The trainer sponged the fighter's stinging eyes and urged him to stay out of Liston's way. Blinking like crazy, Cassius managed to avoid the worst blows until his vision cleared.

Round six: Cassius was back on form with almost every punch finding its target. When the round ended, Liston walked back to his corner, his face a bleeding mess.

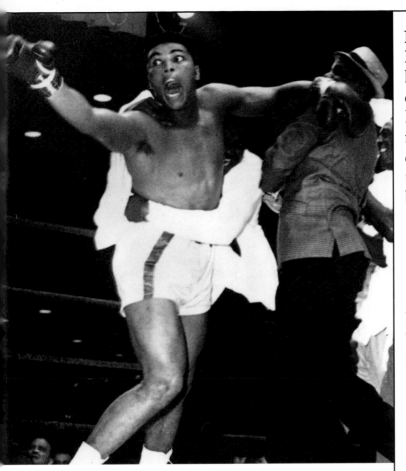

Eat your words
Most reporters had predicted an easy win for Liston. Some found it hard to admit in print that they had been so wrong.

Liston's defeat
Trainers were shocked when Liston refused to fight on. Although he had a sore shoulder and some cuts, he had not been knocked down once.

The bell rang for round seven, but Liston spat out his mouthpiece and refused to leave his corner. Cassius had won.

Ecstatic, he bounded around the ring. "I am the king!" he shouted, and added for the reporters who had not rated his chances – "Eat your words!"

What's in a name?

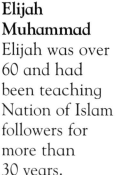

Elijah Muhammad
Elijah was over 60 and had been teaching Nation of Islam followers for more than 30 years.

Cassius's victory stunned the boxing world, but there were more shocks in store. The next day, Cassius confirmed rumors that he had joined the Nation of Islam, a Muslim group led by a man named Elijah Muhammad.

Then he changed his name to Muhammad Ali, a Muslim name meaning "one worthy of praise."

Ali in his Nation of Islam uniform talks to a group of Muslim women called the Sisters of Islam.

Why did Cassius change his name? Like many black people in the US, he had inherited the name given to his great-grandfather by a slave owner, and his first task as a Nation of Islam member was to lose this "slave name." But the press reacted with outrage, describing him as "racist" and "un-American."

Ali was not surprised by the reaction. He had been interested in the Muslim group for years, but he knew that when he joined them he would lose income and popularity.

Members of the Nation of Islam were regarded with suspicion because they believed that black people should find their own strength, separate from white people. Civil rights campaigners were trying to integrate people of different races.

In spite of Ali's strong beliefs, many years passed before people accepted him as Muhammad Ali.

New names
Ali's holy name was an honor. Most members used X as a last name to replace the unknown African names of their slave ancestors.

Ali's tour
Ali decided to tour Africa to meet with "his true people" in Egypt, Ghana, and Nigeria.

Dr. Martin Luther King
A key figure in the civil rights movement, Dr. King was awarded the Nobel Prize for Peace in 1964.

Threats
Rumors that the Nation of Islam had threatened to kill Liston if he did not lose the match fueled public anger against the group.

Ali was ready for a return fight against Sonny Liston, but promoters found they were being turned down by state after state because of Ali's ties to the Nation of Islam.

Many black Americans rejected Ali's beliefs. Most were Christians who followed Dr. Martin Luther King's teachings that black and white people could live together in harmony.

Finally, a bout was fixed for May 25, 1965, in Lewiston, Maine. Liston had trained hard at first, but in the months of waiting he had lost some of his discipline. The fight had been delayed while Ali had a hernia operation, but now Ali was at the peak of fitness.

At the first bell, Ali began to box in his trademark style. In his own words, he liked to "float like a butterfly and sting like a bee."

One minute into the first round, Ali swung a quick, downward right – so fast it seemed to come from nowhere. Liston crashed onto the mat. Ali screamed at him to "Get up and fight!" But Liston just lay there, face up, arms over his head.

Ali was supposed to step back for the ten-second count but he stayed put. When he finally stepped back, 17 seconds had passed. It was a knockout – Ali was victorious.

Knockouts
When a boxer is knocked to the ground, his opponent has to go to a corner, and the referee begins a ten-second count. If the boxer does not get up during the count, the referee declares a knockout.

25

A different fight

Outside of the ring, Ali was a pacifist and bitterly opposed to war.

At age 18, he had been required by law to register for service in the US army. Seven years later, Ali was called up to join the army.

Over the years, the US had become heavily involved in a war in Vietnam in Southeast Asia. More than a half million US troops had been drafted to help South Vietnam defend itself against attacks by North Vietnam.

As a Muslim, Ali objected to war and asked to be excused from service as a conscientious objector. But his request was denied.

Almost everything Ali said was news, but an off-the-cuff remark about the war made headlines.

"I ain't got no quarrel with the Viet Cong," he said. For Ali, it was the simple truth, but people called him a traitor and a coward. When he refused to apologize, his next fight was canceled.

But thousands of other young men were also protesting against US involvement in Vietnam. By standing up to the government, Ali became a powerful symbol to people who were against the war.

Headline news
When Ali refused the draft, no major newspaper had spoken out against the war. But soon other anti-war protests began to make headlines.

Conscientious objectors
People who were given conscientious objector (CO) status were exempted from military service because of their religious or moral beliefs.

At the induction ceremony to enroll Ali in the US army, the draft board called out "Cassius Marcellus Clay." Ali was supposed to step forward to signify that he had joined the army, but he stayed in line. They called the name again – again Ali didn't budge. He no longer answered to his old name, and he refused to move.

It was unlikely that Ali would have been sent into combat in Vietnam – there were plans for him to give exhibition fights to raise the morale of troops. But Ali was morally opposed to the war. Large numbers of black soldiers were being routinely sent to the most dangerous fighting zones. Ali chose to stand by his convictions and risk a jail term.

In June 1967, a jury found him guilty of violating a military service act and fined him $10,000 and sentenced him to five years in jail. Ali was released while he waited for his appeal to be heard.

The World Boxing Association took away his Heavyweight Championship title, and sportswriters attacked him for his cowardice.

Ali never wavered. He had learned more about Vietnam and began to make speeches against the war on college campuses.

Black soldiers
More than 20 percent of the US combat casualties in Vietnam were black soldiers.

Famous protesters
Actress Jane Fonda was one of a number of celebrities who spoke out against US involvement in Vietnam.

There was no legal reason to prevent Ali from boxing. Yet for three and a half years he was banned from fighting in many states.

Joe Frazier was crowned the new World Heavyweight Champion, even though he had never fought Ali to win the title.

But the world was changing fast. By the end of the 1960s, many people were campaigning for peace and racial equality. Ali's protest was now being viewed in a positive light, and promoters decided it was time to get him back in the ring.

In October 1970, they managed to fix up a bout in Atlanta, Georgia, against a boxer named Jerry Quarry. Ali won with a technical knockout – Quarry was cut over his eye and judged too badly hurt to continue. The world's best boxer was back.

Three rounds into the match, Jerry Quarry's face was so cut and bruised the referee brought the fight to an end.

Free to box

Within weeks, a federal court ruled that the ban on Ali fighting in New York was against the law and Ali was free to return to the ring.

But whom to fight? The first choice was Smokin' Joe Frazier, the man holding the title that, Ali believed, was rightfully his own.

Ali gave Frazier the usual treatment, publicly teasing him and calling him "ugly" and "stupid." But in reality, Ali had never faced such a skillful and determined fighter as Joe Frazier. No one was predicting the outcome.

The bout was set for March 8, 1971, at a famous venue – Madison Square Garden in New York City.

Ali and Frazier The world had been waiting for a title fight between Ali and Smokin' Joe Frazier – boxing's biggest rivals. Both fighters were paid the previously unheard-of fee of $2.5 million.

LIFE

BACKSTAGE WITH ALI AND FRAZIER

BATTLE OF THE CHAMPS

MARCH 5 · 1971 · 50¢

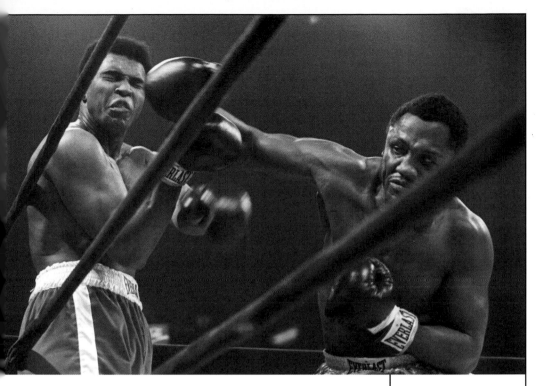

Ali was floating around the ring just out of reach of Frazier's punches. But this time, Ali's own solid punches were failing to make an impact. The two battled it out, round after round.

By the end of the 14th, there was no clear winner. However, in the final round, Ali's strength and speed were abandoning him. Frazier landed a punishing left hook on Ali's jaw and he fell. The Greatest had finally met professional defeat.

Madison Square Garden Many major sports events, including hockey, tennis, and basketball, are staged at the Garden. The world-famous arena also hosts concerts by rock stars and singers, dog and horse shows, and circuses.

Peak years
For most athletes, the years of peak performance are during their twenties. Ali was 25 and at his peak when he was banned from boxing.

Black pride
Black people were showing pride in who they were after years of being treated as inferior. Ali had helped lead the way by calling himself the greatest and the prettiest.

By standing up for his beliefs, Ali had lost his peak years as an athlete, and it was obvious that he was beginning to slow down.

Yet the boxer's defeat by Frazier did nothing to lessen his popularity, especially among young blacks who loved what he represented – black pride, courage, and beauty. Shortly after the Frazier fight, they saw their hero win a different kind of victory.

The Supreme Court voted that Ali was within his rights to refuse the draft. He would not be fined or sent to jail.

Ali was now set on winning back his title, but in the meantime, he met a string of fighters.

One was Ken Norton, a boxer Ali used to practice with. Few fans believed that Norton would win, but early on, he managed to land a hard punch on Ali's jaw, breaking the bone. Ali refused to quit for 11 rounds, but in the 12th, Norton came on strong and won.

Ali went to the hospital with his broken jaw. What was happening to the boxer who had vowed to "stay pretty" and leave the ring unharmed?

Fights
Among his many fights, Ali had a win against Frazier, who had lost the title.

Broken jaw
One of the most common boxing injuries is a broken jaw. Ali's jaw was wired up while it healed.

The "Rumble"

George Foreman
To train for the fight, Foreman told his sparring partners to copy Ali's fast movements while he tried to land punches.

Now Ali had a new contender in his sights – George Foreman, a giant hulk of a man who had taken the heavyweight title from Frazier.

At the request of President Mobutu, a big Ali fan, the title bout was arranged in Zaire (now the Congo) in Africa. The fight was dubbed the "Rumble in the Jungle," and each fighter was promised a $5 million purse – a huge fee.

Ali (right) meets President Mobutu in a scene from the film When We Were Kings.

On October 30, 1974, the "rumble" was set for four o'clock in the morning so US fans could watch the fight live in the evening via closed-circuit TV.

Ali had been told to stay back from Foreman because his thunderous blows usually ended a match in a few rounds. But each time Foreman drew back his arm for a long punch, Ali got a jab in first.

Then commentators were puzzled because Ali kept leaning back on the ropes. This was Ali's new technique – a move that later became known as the "rope-a-dope." Foreman was wearing himself out trying to get to Ali.

Finally, Ali grabbed Foreman's head and whispered, "Hit harder! Show me something, George!"

In the eighth round, Foreman fell to the mat. At age 32, Ali had won back the World Heavyweight title.

Fight story
Film footage of the "Rumble in the Jungle" was made into a documentary film called *When We Were Kings*.

Boxers' purses
The $5 million purse was the largest in boxing history. Ali gave his share to a charity. Today boxers make over $20 million for a heavyweight title fight.

Exhibition fights
Boxers often take part in exhibition fights, lasting only two or three rounds, to help them stay in shape and in the public eye. No winner or loser is declared in these fights.

Ali fought a succession of non-title and exhibition fights, but what the public really wanted to see was a bout between Ali and Frazier – two evenly matched boxers who would guarantee a good fight.

Both boxers had only a few fights left in them. Ali figured he could beat Smokin' Joe one more time before he retired. Frazier thought a win over Ali would be a great way to finish his career.

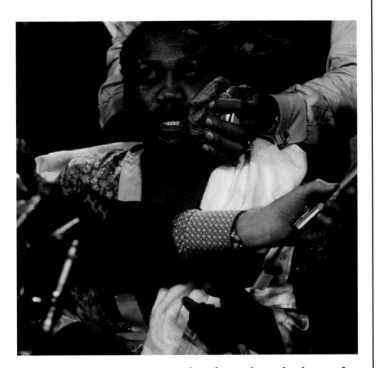

Manila
The Philippines is a scattering of over 7,000 islands in the Pacific Ocean in Southeast Asia. Manila is the main port on the largest island of Luzon.

Plans were made for the fight of the century in the Philippines in September 1975. Dubbed the "Thrilla in Manila," the bout was fought in a steaming 118° F (48° C) between two boxers who refused to give in.

Both fighters received punishing blows. Finally, when Frazier's face was swollen, his mouthpiece gone, and one eye puffed shut, the referee called off the fight. Ali won with a technical knockout, but the fight took a huge toll on both men.

Ms. Ali v Ms. Frazier
The Ali-Frazier rivalry lives on in their boxing daughters, Laila Ali and Jacqui Frazier-Lynde. They met in the ring in June 2001, and Laila Ali won.

Time to stop
A boxer's brain suffers damage through years of punches. Ali once said that young boxers don't like to look at scarred older fighters because they might see their own future.

Leon Spinks
Once a light heavyweight boxer and Olympic gold medal winner, Spinks became notorious for his lavish lifestyle.

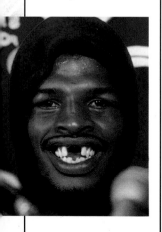

Ali had always insisted that boxers didn't have to get hit. That may have been true in his early days when his lightning-quick reactions kept him dancing away from his opponent's fists. But when he returned to the ring in 1970, Ali had lost much of that speed. He learned that he could take a punch, but there are only so many hits a boxer can take before it begins to affect body and mind.

Although Ali had planned to retire after his victory over Frazier, he was persuaded to go on. He lost his title in February 1978 to underdog Leon Spinks in Las Vegas. Then he won the title back for the third time six months later and decided it was time to retire.

Two years later, managers who should have known better got Ali back into the ring. Was it pride, or money, or simply love of his sport?

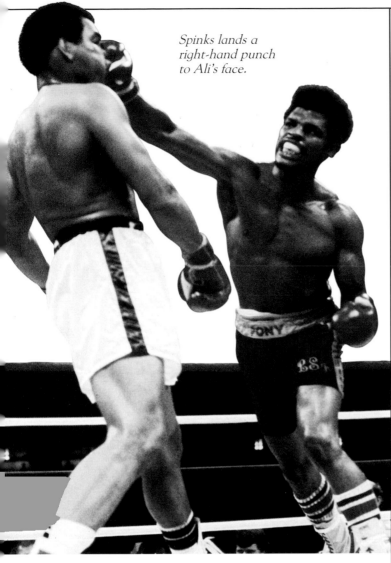

Spinks lands a right-hand punch to Ali's face.

Overweight
Ali was about nine pounds (four kilograms) over his normal fighting weight for his last fight, and it was clear that he was out of condition.

Muhammad Ali Boulevard
Right at the end of Ali's boxing career, Louisville decided to honor him by renaming a city street Muhammad Ali Boulevard.

In the fall of 1980, Ali fought Larry Holmes in Las Vegas and lost. A year later, an overweight and underpowered Ali fought his last fight, against Trevor Berbick, and lost a ten-round decision. He ended his career with 56 wins and 5 losses.

Parkinson's
An English physician named James Parkinson first described the symptoms of a disease called "Shaking Palsy" in 1817. In the 1960s, doctors began to understand how Parkinson's disease affects the brain.

The fight of his life

A year after his last fight, Ali was showing early symptoms of Parkinson's disease, an illness that reduces a vital chemical called dopamine in the brain. Like many people with the disease, Ali began to suffer from trembling hands, body stiffness, and slowed speech. His face began to lose its expression. There is no cure for Parkinson's, although drugs help to reduce its effects.

No one knows for sure whether boxing is to blame for Ali's condition, but there is no denying that many boxers have suffered from brain damage in later life.

Nevertheless, more than one million Americans have the same illness as Ali, and most are not fighters. One is actor Michael J. Fox, who developed Parkinson's at the peak of his career. He now campaigns with Ali to improve understanding of the disease.

Typically, Ali refuses to give in to Parkinson's and talks with honesty and openness about what has happened to him.

As with every battle in his life, Ali is facing this one with courage and great dignity.

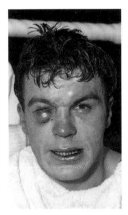

History of the flame
Torch lighting relays were held in Ancient Greece, but it was not until the 1930s that the lighting of a flame became an official part of the Olympic Games.

Ali's torch
Later that night, Ali sat in a chair back at the hotel still holding his Olympic torch. Ali's wife, Lonni, said it was as if he had won the heavyweight title for a fourth time.

The flame burns on

On a warm midsummer night in 1996, the eyes of the world were on Atlanta, Georgia. The Olympic Games arena was full, and three billion people were watching on TV.

Floodlights swept the dark arena and settled on a lone figure in white, holding a torch at center stage. It was Ali, the boxer who had captured the world's attention at the Olympic Games 36 years earlier.

Ali's face could no longer show much emotion, yet this was one of the most exciting moments of his life. With a trembling arm, he reached out to light the Olympic flame. The Games were open.

The crowd rose to its feet, cheering madly. It was a moment of sheer joy for millions of fans and for Ali, too. He was being welcomed back to the most revered athletic competition in the world.

Multimedia Ali

Two decades after Ali left the ring, *Sports Illustrated* and *USA Today* voted him Athlete of the Twentieth Century. Boxing may no longer be as popular as it once was, but those who saw Ali in his prime remember an athlete who brought grace and incredible skill to what is regarded by some as a brutal sport.

Today, children born long after Ali's career ended can get to know a "virtual" Ali, who floats like a butterfly and stings like a bee in a computer game. They can also watch Hollywood actor Will Smith playing Ali in a new movie.

Meanwhile, the real Muhammad Ali attends events around the world and lives peacefully with his family on a 100-acre farm in Michigan.

Athlete of the Century
Ali's own vote went to another champion boxer, Sugar Ray Robinson. "Better than me," Ali said.

Family man
Now married to his fourth wife, Lonni, Ali is the father of seven girls and two boys.

The former champ's favorite place to be is in his gym, where the walls are lined with pictures of his greatest bouts. Ali jokes with visitors that he is planning a comeback, but these days his only fights are against world poverty and injustice. Ali puts the world's great affection for him to good use by fund-raising for charities.

"I hope I can encourage people to show the same love and respect for each other," he says. "If so, it would be a better world."

Honors
Ali was given an honorary degree for his athletic achievement and charitable work. He was also named a United Nations Messenger of Peace.

Ali – the movie
Actor Will Smith worked out for his role with Ali's former trainer. Smith had to eat seven meals a day and drink unlimited protein milk shakes.

Glossary

Black pride
A movement seeking equality for black people and promoting pride in their color and culture.

Bout
A boxing match or competition.

Civil rights movement
A campaign to end conditions of inequality, and to win equal rights for all people.

Communist
A country or person that supports communism – a political movement based on the idea that private ownership should be abolished, and society's resources should be shared equally.

Dopamine
A chemical in the brain that helps nerve cells communicate.

Draft
A legal requirement for a person to join up for military service.

Federal Court
A US court of law dealing with violations of national rather than state laws.

Honorary degree
A symbolic award given to honor the achievements of a person outside of a university or college.

Integration
Moves to help different racial or religious groups live together in harmony (*see* Segregation).

Knockout
A knockout is awarded when a boxer is knocked down and fails to get up within ten seconds.

Liniment
A liquid rubbed on the skin to relieve pain.

Mouthpiece
A plastic guard worn over the teeth to protect them.

Muslim
A person who follows the religion of Islam. Beliefs are based on the Koran, a sacred book that Muslims believe was given by God (Allah) to his prophet Mohammad.

Nation of Islam
A black Muslim group that follows the religion of Islam (*see* Muslim).

Professional (athletes)
Athletes who are paid for taking part in their sport.

Purse
The fee paid to each boxer in a match.

Rounds
Three-minute periods of boxing after which the boxers go to their corners.

Segregation
The separation of people on the basis of race, religion, or color.

Slaves
People who are bought and sold to do unpaid work, and who are denied legal and human rights.

Sparring
Practice fighting using light blows.

Supreme Court
The highest court in the US, possessing the power to uphold or overrule decisions made in lower courts.

Technical knockout
This is awarded when a referee or doctor stops a fight because a boxer is no longer fit to continue.

Underdog
A competitor who is considered unlikely to win a contest.

Viet Cong
A Communist-led guerrilla force and revolutionary army supported by the North Vietnamese.

Vietnam
A country in Southeast Asia, which was divided into North Vietnam and South Vietnam between 1954 and 1976.

Index